TRUMPET

TONS of TUNES

FROM THE CLASSICS

AMY ADAM
MIKE HANNICKEL

CURNOW MUSIC

EXCLUSIVELY DISTRIBUTED BY

HAL•LEONARD
CORPORATION

7777 W. BLUEMOUND RD. P.O. BOX 13819 MILWAUKEE, WI 53213

Edition Number: CMP 1168-07

Amy Adam, Mike Hannickel
TONS OF TUNES from the Classics
Trumpet

CD number: 19-087-3 CMP
CD arrangements by James L. Hosay

ISBN-10: 90-431-2581-4
ISBN-13: 978-90-431-2581-9

© Copyright 2007 by Curnow Music Press, Inc.
P.O. Box 142, Wilmore KY 40390, USA

ARRANGERS

MIKE HANNICKEL grew up in the Sacramento, California area and attended California State University, Sacramento and the University of Southern California. He has been a music teacher in Rocklin, California since 1973. He also composes and publishes exclusively with Curnow Music Press, with whom he has dozens of pieces of music in print.

AMY ADAM was raised in Grand Rapids, Minnesota and attended the University of Minnesota, Duluth graduating with a BM in band education and Flute performance. She has been a music teacher in California since 1992 and currently teaches in Rocklin, California.

TONS OF TUNES

TONS OF TUNES FROM THE CLASSICS is filled with familiar melodies that musicians love to play. The Renaissance, Baroque, Classical, Romantic and Late Romantic periods are all represented in this delightful collection. All the pieces have been arranged in easy keys for wind instruments. The **professional quality accompaniment CD** can be used for practice and performance. You may also choose to purchase the separate easy Piano accompaniment part.

TO MUSIC TEACHERS AND STUDENTS:
TONS OF TUNES FROM THE CLASSICS is perfect for use in Recitals, Talent Shows, Portfolio Demonstrations, Concerts, Private Lessons, and for fun at home. **TONS OF TUNES FROM THE CLASSICS** can be useful in meeting NATIONAL and STATE STANDARDS for music education. All **TONS OF TUNES FROM THE CLASSICS** books can be used alone or together so any group of musicians can play as an ensemble.

TO THE MUSICIAN:
Whether you recognize these melodies from the concert hall, CDs, movies, or cartoons; you are sure to be familiar with many of them. Have **FUN** playing them with family and friends! If you have different types of instruments, you can still play together. Each person needs to get the **TONS OF TUNES FROM THE CLASSICS** book for their instrument.

FROM THE CLASSICS
CONTENTS

TONS OF TUNES
FROM THE CLASSICS

TRUMPET

Arr. by Amy Adam and
Mike Hannickel (ASCAP)

1. Humming Song

Robert Schumann (1810-1856)

2. Bransle de champaigne

Gervaise (ca.1550)

3. Musette

J.S.Bach (1685-1750)

4. See, the Conquering Hero Comes

George Frideric Handel (1685-1759)

5. Fanfare

Michel Corrette (1709-1795)

6. Bouffons

Thoinot Arbeau (1520-1595)

7. Theme from "Pathetique"

Ludwig van Beethoven (1770-1827)

8. Rondo Alla Turca

Wolfgang Amadeus Mozart
(1756-1791)

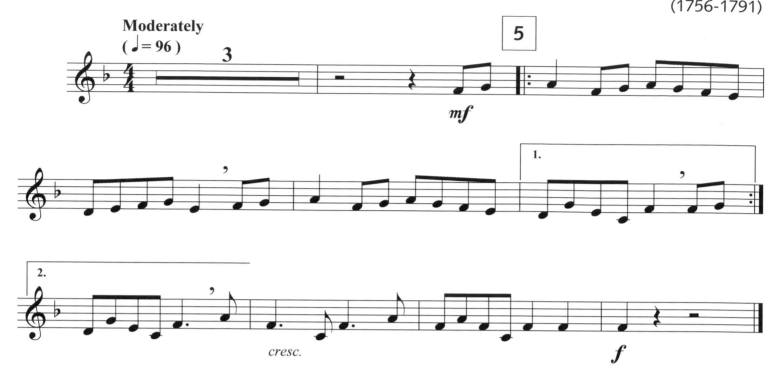

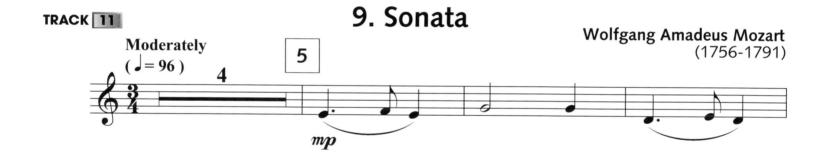

9. Sonata

Wolfgang Amadeus Mozart
(1756-1791)

10. Spring

Antonio Vivaldi (1678-1741)

11. Scherzo

Muzio Clementi (1752-1832)

12. Scottish Dance

Ludwig van Beethoven
(1770-1827)

1168-07 CMP • Trumpet

13. Minuet

J.S.Bach (1685-1750)

14. William Tell Overture

Gioachino Rossini
(1792-1868)

15. Lullaby

Johannes Brahms (1833-1897)

16. Funeral March

Frederic Chopin (1810-1849)

17. Pomp And Circumstance

Sir Edward Elgar (1857-1934)

18. Trumpet Voluntary

Jeremiah Clarke (1674-1707)

Moderately fast
(♩ = 116)

TRACK 21

19. "Largo" from The New World

Antonin Dvorak (1841-1904)

Slowly
(♩ = 82)

13

21

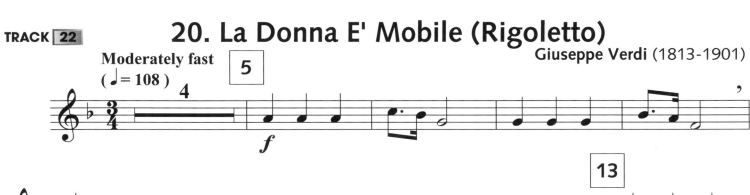

TRACK **22**

20. La Donna E' Mobile (Rigoletto)

Giuseppe Verdi (1813-1901)

Moderately fast
(♩ = 108)

5

13

21

21. On The Beautiful Blue Danube

Johann Strauss (1825-1899)

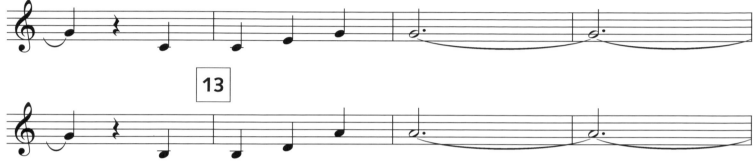

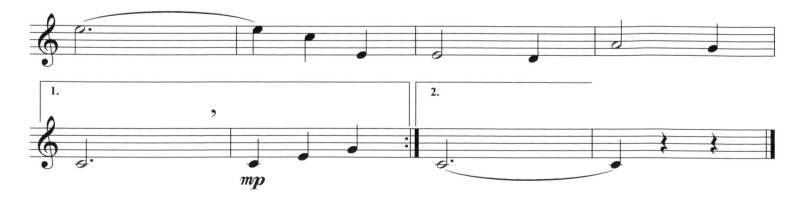

22. The Anvil Chorus (Il Trovatore)

Giuseppe Verdi (1813-1901)

23. Humoresque

Antonin Dvorak (1841-1904)

24. Spring

Felix Mendelssohn (1809-1847)

25. Farandole

Georges Bizet (1838-1875)

26. Morning

Edvard Grieg (1843-1907)

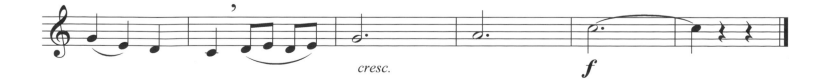

27. Rondeau

Jean-Joseph Mouret (1682-1738)

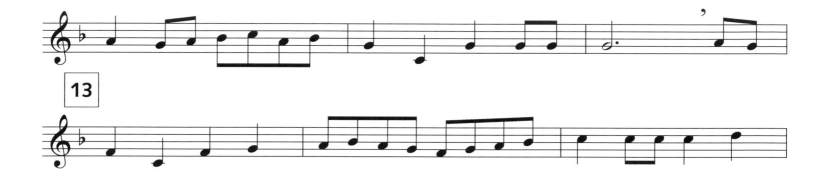

13

21

25

28. Hungarian Dance #5

Johannes Brahms (1833-1897)

29. Toreador Song

Georges Bizet (1838-1875)

30. Hallelujah Chorus

George Frideric Handel (1685-1759)

31. Trumpet Tune

Henry Purcell (1659-1695)

13

32. Fur Elise

Ludwig van Beethoven (1770-1827)

14

Rall.